AF104238

Your Best Survival Guide on Sleep Training Your Baby
A Guide to Giving Your Baby the Gift of Sleep Through Breathing Techniques, Healthy Habits, and Relaxation Methods.
By: Kelly Curtiss

Introduction

Tired? Frustrated? Is your baby's cries ringing in your ears even when you're sleeping? Do you even know what day it is?

If your eyes are too exhausted to keep reading, then you definitely need this book! This is for all the tired moms and dads out there who just want five precious minutes of uninterrupted sleep.

Today is your lucky day because I am about to introduce you to several methods that can get you a few hours of uninterrupted and much-needed sleep. A baby is precious, and these are moments that you want to be able to enjoy for as long as you can. You can't enjoy your baby if you are constantly sleep deprived. That is a simple fact. You also do not want to have to give your baby anything external to make them sleep just so that you can catch up on all those sleepless nights.

This guide is meant to help you find some great methods that can work for you and your baby! Everyone needs a good night's rest. That includes you and your baby. So, dive into this book and let us provide you a method that will work for your routine. Sleep training is a very rewarding process.

I look forward to helping you discover new ways to tackle your sleepless baby. Who knows, at the end of this guide you might even find yourself snoozing away!

Chapter One: What Is Sleep Training?

Sleep training goes by several names, and it is often also referred to as sleep training. It is simply the method that you use to teach your baby to fall asleep and stay asleep. Does this sound like heaven to you? Good! Sleep training can be a controversial topic, simply because there are so many different ways that you can train your baby to fall asleep. Keep in mind that there is no ONE perfect way to sleep train your baby, and that is why there are so many different methods. Every parent and infant combination is going to be unique and different from the last. So, give yourself time and do your best to block out those who want you to follow their methods while you have a way that works for your family.

Sleep is critical to your baby's health and development. This is one of the biggest benefits you can get from sleep training. However, it goes beyond just your baby's health. Your peace of mind and sanity are on the line here too. You need to sleep in order to function properly and be the best parent you can to your baby. This is why even the National Institute of Health suggests and promotes that you help your baby sleep and guide them into a method that works for you. As your baby sleeps they are developing critical brain functions and pathways, and this brain development can't be gained through any other methods. Sleep training might not be the most fun you ever had with your baby, but it will be the most beneficial and peaceful!

Keep in mind that sleep training will not work for everyone. Just because you don't sleep train does not mean that eventually, your child will not learn to sleep on their own. It is a trial and error process that you and your family need to decide if it is right for you. You should not feel pressured into training your baby into any particular method of sleep training. Some people have great success through not sleep training, others need sleep training in order to regain some composure and normalcy in their lives.

Infants are dependent entirely on you, and so it is your job to find out what will work best for your family. Sleep training does not hurt so, where is the harm in trying it? If it works then great! You and your family have bought yourselves a one-way ticket to a lot of restful nights. I can only wish you luck as you embark on this journey. Please remember that sleep training can be incredibly rewarding.

Chapter Two: Sleep Training Misconceptions and Myths

With sleep training come the inevitable myths and misconceptions that surround almost every parenting technique in the world. Sometimes it can be hard to think through the myths and old wives tales that we are being told. That is why below I have compiled some of the most common myths that exist and I will talk you through them. Don't let a misconception ruin a great thing for you and your baby.

The Myth that Crying it Out Can Damage Your Baby

There are many people out there who continue to perpetuate the myth that crying it out can hurt your baby. Let me be clear before we go any further on this topic: crying it out does not, will not, and cannot harm your baby or their development. There have been numerous scientifically led experiments that have shown the same results with the cry it out method time and time again. It just does not hurt your baby and no evidence has ever pointed to the contrary.

This is not to say that this method works for everyone because it does not. This is not the best method for everyone and it is certainly not a one all solve all technique. However, it has had great success and some families still use it to train their infants because it works.

Throw away the rumors that circulate through all the parenting circles and focus on the facts of this case. The American Academy of Pediatrics Journal has even released a study where they show that not only is the cry it out method successful in sleep training, but there is no damage to the brain or a stunt in emotional growth. See? The research speaks for itself. As for you, you just need to put aside the hearsay and find out what works for you and your baby.

The Myth That Says If They Wake Up at Night They Need You

As great as it feels to be needed, just because your baby wakes up in the middle of the night does not mean that they need you. This myth can be put to bed with the simple fact that your baby is learning to move during their sleep. Motor function develops while your baby is both awake and asleep, and sometimes as they are developing these functions they do wake themselves up. This can be caused by a simple leg or hand twitch. Your baby does not always need you when they wake up - even if they are crying. Sometimes it is as simple as their cry meaning they need more sleep. Try your best not to fuss over them when they wake up during the night. Pay attention to their needs. No one knows your baby better than you do. You will know if they are hungry or if they are just tired. Relax; you guys have this in the bag.

The Myth That You Should Keep Them Awake in the Day to Sleep Better

This is probably one of the most popular misconceptions that exist involving sleep training. It seems fairly simple and straightforward. If you keep your baby up during the day then they will want to sleep during the night. Unfortunately, I have to burst this bubble today. It is simply not true. Your baby needs their naps because their energy bursts will require them to sleep through several periods in order to be rested and have the energy to be awake, eat, drink, and play later on.

Here is where this plan will really kick you in the butt. Adults get really tired the longer we stay up and keep ourselves entertained. By the time our bedtime approaches, we are ready to hit the sack. This is not true for infants. Babies will go into a mode called hyperactivity. This means that they are so tired they cannot sleep and the result is a baby who seems to be throwing tantrums, crying and bouncing off the walls for no reason in particular. When you keep your baby up all day and deprive them of their much-needed sleep you are asking for a meltdown during bedtime. Save yourself, your family, and your baby undue headaches and keep them on their napping schedule. It is not worth keeping them awake all day.

The Myth That Sleep Training Takes A Long Time

Sleep training does not have to take months or years. I promise you that anyone who has told you this has not stuck to their methods of sleep training (we will go over this in more detail as you keep reading). Sleep training has been known to take as few as two nights up to a few weeks. The reason that the timing for sleep training varies so much is due to the individual baby and family. Remember, not everyone is the same so; you can't measure your progress or success by someone else's results. If your baby is around four months or older the chances are high that in just two weeks of sleep training you will have a baby who lets you catch up on all that missed sleep too.

Give yourself and your baby the time that you guys need to make sleep training work. It is important because sleep is not a resource that we can decide if we need or not - our bodies will crash and the immune system will be compromised by a lack of sleep. So, stick it out, focus on the good times to come ahead.

The Myth That You Can Take a Break From Sleep Training

I want to expand on this particular myth. This is where a lot of well-meaning parents fail and struggle with sleep training. You cannot take a break from sleep training and expect to pick back where you left off. Sleep training needs consistency. This means that you need to be consistent with the where, when, and how. Even though your baby is still young, they like the routine that you have set up for them. So, when you set up and stick to a routine involving sleep training you are much more likely to have success then if you stopped in the middle of training. I know it can be frustrating when it seems like on method is not working out for you, but don't change it up every few nights. Give them a week or two to get used to the new routine before you throw in the towel. Research has proven that behavioral sleep issues can be solved one hundred percent of the time. The times that fail means that we are doing something wrong in the routine. Do your best to be consistent while you sleep training; it pays off in the long run.

Chapter Three: Simple Methods to Sleep Train Your Baby

Sleep training your baby becomes a lot easier when you are able to employ a method that works for you. Do you remember when I said that there is more than one way to sleep train a baby? Well, here they are! There are lots of different methods that involve sleep training that will help you and your family get the rest that you deserve.

No Tears

The sleep expert Elizabeth Pantley created this method. It is also commonly called the "no cry method." The use of this technique slowly changes the sleep habits that your baby or child has adopted. There are several tricks that come under the blanket of the *No Tears* method. Firstly, you can try to "fade" your baby. This involves taking away the comforts that they are used to falling asleep one by one. So, if you have a baby who only falls asleep when you rock them, each night that you are sleep training you need to rock them less and less. Eventually, if you stay diligent with this you should be able to put them down without needed to rock them at all. The other method within this No Tears method is to try and substitute your baby's regular routine. This can mean if they are used to you being given a bottle before bed, read them a book instead and then put them to sleep. The objective is to gently coax your baby or child to get used to sleeping on their own without the comforts that was your crutch before.

Cry It Out

The infamous cry-it-out method is the subject of many debates in the parenting community, but despite the old wives tales that surround this method it is highly effective in getting your child to sleep on their own. The object of this method is to allow your baby to learn to comfort itself. Instead of rushing in every time they have a need or they cry, let them cry it out on their own until they fall asleep.

This method can be difficult for many parents to accomplish because we have been led to believe that we should rush in to soothe a crying baby. I promise you that after a few nights of this method, your baby will manage to comfort itself. The first few nights can be trying on a parent's nerves, but just keep in mind what I said about consistency. It is the key to sleep training.

The Weissbluth Method

This method may sound like a mouthful, but it has its merit. With this method, the premise is to set up a nighttime routine for your baby that prepares them for bed. This can take the form of giving them a bath, reading them a book, and then singing them a lullaby as they prepare for bed. Once you put the baby to bed you need to close the door and remain out of their room until the next morning. This method can be another hard one for parents to do since the instinct to run into the room when your baby is awake can be overwhelming. Each night your baby will cry less and less as they get used to their routine for bed. They will come to expect it and soon they will be sleeping throughout the night.

The Ferber Method

The Ferber method employs the use of timing your sleep training. This is most commonly done through timed intervals but can be modified to suit individual parental needs. The Ferber method asks you to put your baby to sleep (crying or not crying) and set a timer in which you can come check on them. Start out slow and check on your baby every five minutes. It is important to remember that you are just doing a check here and you are not supposed to pick the baby up; you can, however, talk to them to calm them or pat their back lightly.

As you check up on them less infrequently (expanding your intervals to every ten to fifteen minutes and even longer into hours) you will find that their sleeping patterns remain more consistent over time.

The Chair Method

The Chair Method is more commonly known as gradual withdrawal. While she is not the inventor of the method, Kim West is behind the popularization of this method. She wrote Good Night, Sleep Tight, which explains the method. First, you should place your baby in their crib and pull a chair up next to them. The first night you stay right by your baby and soothe them and help them to sleep. The next night you should place your chair just a little further away. Each night moving further away in a process of gradual withdrawal. As you move further away and your baby cries, you will resort to only verbally soothing them to get them down again. Eventually, you will be out of the room completely and your baby will be able to sleep without your presence because they slowly got used to you being further away during bedtime. This method is great for babies and young children who have separation anxiety as it teaches them that you are still there for them even if you are not in the room.

The Pick-Up and Put Down Method

This method is very similar to the Ferber method in that you set regularly timed intervals to check in on your baby. Where it differs from the Ferber method is that it allows you to pick up your baby when you check on them. Pick them up and comfort them (only during your interval to check on them) and then put them back to sleep. Soon your baby will feel comfortable sleeping on their own as you expand the time between checks.

Chapter Four: Make Sleep Training Work for You

Sleep Training and Meditation

Meditation and children might sound like it does not go hand in hand, but have a little faith. Meditation in children will not look like it does in adults. Using meditation to relax your child into sleep works best on older children, but if you have a baby you can easily facilitate some of the meditation techniques onto them. You will use meditative techniques to soothe and calm them into a relaxed state so that their body wants to sleep.

Meditation works best for children and babies who have a bedtime routine. For example, if they brush their teeth, change into their pajamas and then have had their stories read to them, they can easily adjust to adding meditation into their nighttime routine. It will also help you, as the parent, be more consistent with the techniques.

- Meditation should be a point in the bedtime routine where you connect with your child or baby. You can have them quietly talk to you about their day, their fears or concerns, and their thoughts. This helps them expel all the thoughts on their mind and gets them in a state where they are ready to meditate.
- Make meditating fun for your child, and show them that you are doing it with them. Breathe deeply in, and then exhale by making a weird sound (animal sounds are always a big hit).
- As your child exhales, place their hands on their stomach so they can feel their own body rising and falling while they breathe in and out. For a baby, you can simply place your hand on their tummy and breathe in and out to match their breathing.
- Once they get into the rhythm of breathing, put on a calm song and have them focus on just their breathing for the duration of the song.
- Sometimes guided meditation books can help you facilitate this

process for your child. Pick books that are geared towards children like "A Handful of Quiet" and "Mindful Monkey." These are great resources to help get your child into the practice of meditation and also help them sleep better through the night.

- Be patient. It takes time and consistency for any great change to take place, so bear with it and don't throw in the towel on the first night. This is a great time for you to relax your own body and mind.

What NOT to do When Sleep Training

There is so much information out there regarding sleep training that sometimes we forget the basics. Yes, there are myths to sleep training, and there are also some amazing methods to use to sleep train. However, there are also a few common no-nos that you do not want to incorporate into your sleep training habits.

Rock or Feed Your Baby to Sleep

Feeding and rocking your baby before bed can be a common trap that many parents fall into. This is mainly because during your baby's first few months, eating and rocking are pretty much what they need. With the exception of the one billion and three diaper changes, they need as well. In the first few months of your baby's life, this is totally normal behavior, but as they near that four-month mark you want them to start developing healthy sleep routines.

You do not want feeding and rocking to be the only way you can get your child to sleep, especially if they wake up several times in the night. That means that the three to six times they wake up you have to get up to feed or rock them because they are used to that routine.

The simplest way to fix this is to find a new bedtime routine and get your baby adjusted to expecting this routine before bed. When you start a new routine, they will get used to that and will no longer rely on the rocking or feeding to go to sleep.

Do Not Pick Your Baby Up Every Time They Cry

Learning the difference between when to comfort your crying child and when to let them cry it out can be an extremely fine line to walk on. It is recommended that during the first six months of your baby's life that you do comfort them and go to them when they cry so that they can expect to rely on you. The only caution is to wait a few minutes before rushing in to see why they are crying. Often times your baby will settle back down again - particularly if they are simple whimpering - and you will not have to rush into the room to tend to their imaginary upset. The reason you do not want to pick them up whenever they cry is that as they grow older they will begin to realize that this is an instant way to get attention or the easiest way to what they want.

To stop yourself from running into the room every time the baby cries, try asking yourself if you have met all of their needs. Are they fed? Is their diaper changed? Are they sick? This will help you eliminate why they might really be crying. If they are only crying because you are no longer in the room then you should try a gradual withdrawal method with them where they get used to sleeping without your direct presence in the room. It is important to remember that when your baby cries they are learning. Part of the lessons they need to learn is how to comfort themselves, you are not depriving your child if they cry and you wait three minutes to answer their cries.

Napping throughout the Day

Sometimes it is easy to let your baby sleep while you go to the bank or the grocery store. If they are napping that means that they are not fussing. The problem with this is they become used to sleeping with movement, and therefore will later find it hard to fall asleep if they are not in motion.

Your baby needs consistent nap times and a designated nap area. If your day is organized so that she naps in her crib where most of her sleeping is done then you have an easier chance of keeping her routine as regular as possible. This will not work every day, but try to stick to it as much as you possibly can.

Do Not Let Your Baby Stay Up Late at Night

Babies do not know when they need to sleep and when they need to be awake. For this, they rely on you to guide and train them. Sometimes it is tempting to let your baby stay awake until they possibly can't keep their eyes open anymore, but you will only create a nightmare for yourself. The longer it takes your baby to fall asleep, the more frequently they will wake up throughout the day. As babies get overtired they become overly sensitive, irritable and moody.

You should try your best to have your baby fall into a regular bedtime schedule because by the time they are four or five months old they should be going to sleep around seven or eight o'clock at night. If your baby is used to going to bed late at night, coax them to bed earlier every night by a period of 15 or 20 minutes until you have reached seven o'clock.

Chapter Five: Techniques that Stick So You Can Sleep

Sleep training is not always a walk in the park, and sometimes even when you have a routine down something can knock it right off of its path. There will be times when you take a few steps back from the progress you have made, this is inevitable with life. Sicknesses happen, teething begins, vacations go on and all of these change your baby's regular routine. Just know that this is okay, you are still doing great! There is nothing wrong with circling back to sleep training methods to get your baby or child back onto their routine.

Do It Yourself Methods Work

Here is the great thing about sleep training: it is one hundred percent flexible! If one method does not work for you or is particularly too rigid for you then you can change it to match the needs of you and your baby. Don't feel constrained to do a method a particular way, because there is more than one way to get your baby to sleep peacefully through the night.

If you feel like you need help coming up with a plan, reach out to a sleep coach who will help you find what works best for your family and your schedule. Sometimes you need to improvise to make it fit with you and that is absolutely okay. As long as you are patient and consistent you should achieve the same results!

Don't Quit

Sleep training can be hard, especially when their tiny baby cries pierce through your heart. But don't give in. Don't throw in the towel yet. Prepare yourself for the hard times. Tell yourself ahead of time that this journey won't be easy but it will definitely be worth it. Just because your baby cries the first week of their sleep training does not mean they will never be trained. Remember, it can take up to four weeks to train your baby to sleep through the night. If you feel like you have given a particular method your best shot (and by this, I mean more than one week of trying), try a new one by slowly introducing it into your schedule. It is perfectly okay to mix things up if they are not working.

Never Compare Your Progress to Others

It can be completely disheartening to see or hear about others doing better than you are with sleep training their child. Do not fall into this route. You are doing a great job; every baby is unique and will progress at their own rates. If you judge yourself and your baby off of other people's needs then you are not giving yourself a real chance to sleep train your baby in ways that meet your needs. What works for one person will not work for the next, so comparisons need to go out the window.

Stick to That Bedtime Routine

I know I have spoken a lot about routine, but I really want you to understand the importance and crucial difference that a good routine can make in your sleep training. If you keep things consistent and make sure that your baby's bedtime remains the same then the odds of your success greatly increase. Keep in mind those meditative techniques that you can use during bedtime as well to soothe your baby to sleep.

Don't worry if you are not ready to start sleep training. Not everyone will be ready at the same time. You will know when it is time to start training your baby to sleep - either when they let you know it is time or you will know when you find out that you put salt in your coffee again instead of sugar.

Sleep training can be rewarding and is not delegated to just infants and babies. Toddlers and even older children benefit greatly from consistent methods with sleep training. There is no shame in admitting that you are struggling with sleep training. This admittance could even be the start of you getting the solutions you need. There are sleep consultants and coaches that exist to fulfill the need that both you and your baby have - SLEEP!

Conclusion

At the end of the day, no routine will work the same for two sets of parents and babies. You will discover the best path that helps you and your baby sleep. You have learned a lot through this guide, and I feel confident that you are now prepared with all the information you need in order to start sleep training your baby.

If you ever feel like you need to go through some more methods, refer back to this book, it can always be used for future sleep training endeavors. You have learned what sleep training is, the myths that surround sleep training and the different methods that you can use to sleep train your baby.

One of the greatest pieces of advice that I can impart to you about sleep training is that it can be easily changed to match your needs and schedule. You never need to feel pigeonholed into one way of doing things. Have fun with it, try and relax yourself as you sleep train your baby, and prepare yourself for their tears. I wish you nothing but the best on this journey, and I am sending calming thoughts your way.

© **Copyright 2019 - All rights reserved.**

The content contained within this book may not be reproduced, duplicated or transmitted without direct written permission from the author or the publisher.

Under no circumstances will any blame or legal responsibility be held against the publisher, or author, for any damages, reparation, or monetary loss due to the information contained within this book. Either directly or indirectly.

<u>Legal Notice:</u>

This book is copyright protected. This book is only for personal use. You cannot amend, distribute, sell, use, quote or paraphrase any part, or the content within this book, without the consent of the author or publisher.

<u>Disclaimer Notice:</u>

Please note the information contained within this document is for educational and entertainment purposes only. All effort has been executed to present accurate, up to date, and reliable, complete information. No warranties of any kind are declared or implied. Readers acknowledge that the author is not engaging in the rendering of legal, financial, medical or professional advice. The content within this book has been derived from various sources. Please consult a licensed professional before attempting any techniques outlined in this book.

By reading this document, the reader agrees that under no circumstances is the author responsible for any losses, direct or indirect, which are incurred as a result of the use of information contained within this document, including, but not limited to, — errors, omissions, or inaccuracies.

www.ingramcontent.com/pod-product-compliance
Lightning Source LLC
LaVergne TN
LVHW020430070526
838199LV00004B/341